RABBIT J_____

How to teach your rabbit to jump

BY

Emma Lundqvist

Contents

Introduction

Are you looking for a fun activity to do with your rabbit? Well, look no further. Using this guide you can get started in a popular sport in many European countries – rabbit jumping!

Rabbit jumping has many similarities to show jumping for horses, which is how it originated. The goal is to jump cleanly over a course of fences within an allotted time frame. The only thing you need to get started is a rabbit and a will to learn. Rabbits are natural jumpers and smarter than many people think. Most of them enjoy the stimulation and attention they get from training with their owner. It's also healthy for them to move outside of their cage and it keeps them in shape.

This is the perfect activity to do with your rabbit if you have been looking for a way to not only exercise and entertain your animal, but also to build a stronger bond with each other.

There are currently federations arranging competitions all over Scandinavia and the interest is growing in Germany, UK and USA as well. If you are unsure if competitions are currently held in your country, do a quick search to find out. If you can't find any competitions in your area, why not organize a small competition amongst friends?

Even if you don't plan on going as far as competing with you rabbit, I will take you through the basic structure of how rabbit jumping works in the country of its origin - Sweden. These are the guidelines that I have based this book on, they have developed during the years to benefit both the rabbit and you, the handler.

Rabbit jumping today

Did you know that the first national championship in rabbit jumping was held way back in 1986? And that the first rabbit jumping club organized their first competitions back in the 70's? Rabbit jumping has been a well-recognized sport in Scandinavia and other parts of Europe for many years. It's not just a sport for young children, ages of members range anywhere from 7 to 70 years.

During the first years, rabbit jumping was largely based on how show jumping for horses work. As the sport grew changes have been made to better suit rabbits.

There are four different disciplines to choose from; straight course, crooked course, high jump and long jump. The names are fairly self-explanatory. For the straight course, which is usually considered the easiest discipline to start with, the fences are placed in a straight line. The crooked course looks more like show jumping for horses, where the fences are placed out with turns and loops in between. There are also different classes ranging from easy to elite where the fences are between 20 to 50 cm high and 30 to 80 cm long depending on the level of difficulty. In the classes called high jump and long jump the rabbit will only jump over one fence. The rabbit who jumps the highest or longest depending on the class will win.

In Sweden there are currently over twenty federations across the nation that are organizing competitions. Norway, Finland and Denmark have followed closely in their footsteps. Other countries where rabbit jumping are increasing in popularity are Germany, United Kingdom and USA. Do a search to see if you can find a federations in your area! Becoming a member in a club and getting hands-on support from likeminded people can be invaluable and very rewarding.

What do you need to get started?

- A rabbit that is at least three months old.
- A harness and a long leash.
- A couple of fences to jump. When starting out you don't need anything fancy, just keep in mind that the fences need to be safe with no nails or sharp edges sticking out that can hurt your rabbit. You should be able to knock down the pole from both directions. Thin plastic PVC pipes are perfect to use for poles since they are so light, but you can also use an old handle from a broom stick or a straight branch from the woods - use your imagination!
- An open space to practice – either outside in your backyard or inside on a carpet so that the rabbit does not slip.

What to consider when buying a rabbit

Maybe you are missing the most important part to be able to start with rabbit jumping – the rabbit itself. Or maybe you are interested in finding a more suitable individual to jump with than the one that you already own. In this chapter I will go through what factors to consider when buying a jumping rabbit.

Before you hand over the money and bring your new rabbit home, there are a few things worth considering. First of all, you need to be aware that rabbits will usually live to be around six to nine years old. If you are not prepared to make such a long commitment, consider finding an adult rabbit instead of a baby. We all know that a baby bunny is one of the cutest creatures out there, so it can be tempting to buy the first little furry friend you lay eyes on. Try to take a step back and ask yourself if you are willing to house an adult rabbit for up to ten years just to be able to enjoy those four to eight weeks of baby bunny cuteness. There are many adult rabbits out there struggling to find a good home, so I would encourage you to look at that as an alternative.

When you have decided to go ahead and buy a rabbit, consider for what reason you are doing it, because it will dictate what breed and gender you should choose. If you want an all-round pet with pleasant temperament as well as a potentially successful jumping rabbit I would suggest some kind of Miniature Lop. They are generally brave, sweet and gentle rabbits which is perfect for both beginners and experienced rabbit owners. If you also want to have the opportunity to show your rabbit you should go with a purebred, but if you only want to be able to compete in rabbit jumping mixes are also permitted. For rabbit jumping, the build of the rabbit is more important than the pedigree. Look for a rabbit that is mid-sized and agile.

There is nothing wrong with going to your local pet store and buying a rabbit from there, some rabbits competing in the highest level in Sweden came from a pet store. If you want to increase your chances of getting a rabbit that likes jumping you should however turn to a breeder specializing in jumping rabbits. Search for breeders near you on the internet or look through ads. Consider checking if there is a rabbit jumping club in your area, they usually list breeders and competitors on their sites and if you get in touch with them they might be able to help you find what you are looking for. Some breeders also have adult rabbit jumpers for sale that have competed previously which of course can be a great help for beginners. That way you don't have to worry about training the rabbit, only yourself.

Which gender to choose depends from person to person. Some people prefer males and others females. Keep in mind that unneutered males must be kept alone, because two male rabbits will usually fight each other if they meet. Males can also be quite territorial and if you are unlucky, your rabbit might want to mark his scent by urinating on things. Neutering the rabbit will usually help. Females can be kept together if they have a large enough cage but some females can get very uncooperative when they are in heat, especially in the spring time. There are pro's and con's with both genders so weigh them against each other and pick the one that you prefer. Both males and females can become successful jumpers. If you are planning on breeding your rabbit in the future, it could be an advantage to start with a female. That way you can choose to borrow a male to breed with your rabbit, without having to actually buy another rabbit.

So let's say that you have decided what breed and gender to buy, from where you will buy it and also whether it will be a baby or an adult. The next step is to pick your rabbit. I know it is tempting to choose the rabbit with the coolest color or cutest eyes, but try to consider the temperament. Look for a brave rabbit that doesn't seem to get startled easily. Try to avoid the rabbit sitting far back in the cage and look instead for the one that is active and seeks out contact with people. Even if the rabbit has not been handled a lot previously, it is a good sign if it will accept having people around it. New things should be met with curiosity – not fear.

When you have finally brought your new rabbit home, be sure to give it some time to settle in before you start training.

Before you start jumping

If you expect your rabbit to enjoy and benefit from jumping you will first need to make sure that its basic needs are fulfilled. A happy and satisfied rabbit is much more likely to become a good jumper.

Housing

When you consider how to house your rabbit, you firstly need to choose if you are going to keep your rabbit inside or outside. Rabbits are quite resilient and they like living outside even when the temperature goes well below freezing. If you are keeping your rabbit outside it is especially important that it has access to a small hutch above ground. Make sure that the hutch is filled with generous amounts of dry straw. It does not have to be isolated because the straw will keep your rabbit dry and warm, keeping it off the ground will shelter it from the cold ground as well. If you choose to keep your rabbit inside the hutch is less important. You should however give your rabbit some form of house or shelf that it can sit on, as rabbits often enjoy doing that.

The larger the cage the better is usually the case when it comes to rabbits. They enjoy being able to move around and stay active on their own. For a miniature rabbit the cage will need to be at least 100x50x50 cm or 40x20x20 inches but those are only the minimum requirements. The size of the cage is especially important if you want to keep more than one rabbit. Female rabbits often enjoy living together, but only if they have enough space.

As bedding in the cage people will usually go with wood chippings and/or straw. The cage will need to be cleaned regularly to keep the bedding dry and fresh. Keeping the cage clean will also help with any odors.

Feeding

Rabbits are naturally grass eaters, but normally we will not be able to have our rabbits out eating grass all year round. That is why we resort to dried grass, or hay as it is commonly referred to. This is the main feed for rabbits, as long as they have access to fresh hay and water they will not require much else. If you have an active rabbit or a rabbit who lives outdoor in colder temperatures you may want to give him some pelleted or muesli feed to supplement. Look for a natural rabbit feed that does not contain a high amount of sugar or dried fruit – that should be considered as candy for your rabbit. Rabbits usually only need a small amount of pellets, a few tablespoons a day is enough for a small rabbit. Don't be fooled if your rabbit eats all of the pellets at once, it will have to eat the hay if it's hungry as that should be the main source of food. It can also be good to give your rabbit a few daily vegetables, such as carrots, salad or green peppers. Make sure that you introduce new foods slowly and in small amounts so that your rabbit has time to get used to it.

A rabbits' teeth continues to grow throughout its entire life, that is why it is so important that your rabbit has access to chew on hay all day long. This will keep the teeth from growing too long. It can also be beneficial to give your rabbit some branches to chew on – branches from apple trees are usually especially popular.

Exercise

Rabbits are naturally quite active animals. They will need to move and exercise in order to stay healthy and in good shape. Rabbits who live in small cages will have a greater need for exercise. Rabbits that live inside love to jump around freely in the house and they are usually quiet easily house-trained. Some people keep their rabbits like dogs, letting them have free access to the whole house which of course is ideal. If you do not have that luxury, try to let your rabbit run freely for at least one hour daily.

If you have a backyard you can easily put together a larger pen where your rabbit can leisure, dig in the dirt and eat grass during the summers. Rabbits that live outside often enjoy discovering in the snow as well. If your rabbit lives inside, be careful with taking it outside during the colder months, as your rabbit will not have the proper winter coat to keep itself warm.

If you do not have available space to build a pen outside you can of course also exercise your rabbit in a harness. I will go through how to harness train your rabbit in the coming chapter. If you have your rabbit on a leash you will always need to be there and hold it, never tie your rabbit to something and leave it without supervision. Your rabbit could entangle itself and get hurt.

Making sure that your rabbit gets enough exercise is important when you want to start jumping. A rabbit that is in good condition will not tire as easily and there is also less chance that it will get hurt or strained.

Maintenance

As mentioned before, a rabbits' teeth will continue growing throughout its entire life. Therefor it can be good to check the teeth from time to time to make sure that they look healthy. Some rabbits develop an under- or overbite which will cause their teeth to grow incorrectly. Even though you might be doing everything right with providing your rabbit enough hay and branches to chew on the teeth will not get grinded down properly. This can be something that was passed down genetically or it can be something that developed when your rabbit was growing up. It is very important that you never breed a rabbit that has a faulty bite. In the worst case scenario, your rabbit may end up having difficulty chewing and getting enough nutrition from the food. In those cases a veterinarian can trim the rabbits' teeth manually to keep them appropriate in length.

You will also need to keep an eye on the rabbits' claws. They need to be trimmed down regularly unless your rabbit keeps them in check by digging. Some rabbits can be quite tricky to trim, so it can be helpful to get assistance from somebody. That way one person can hold the rabbit and the other one can trim the claws.

Also keep an eye on your rabbits' general wellbeing. Does the eyes look clear or are they foggy and tired? Is the nose runny? Is your rabbit active, eating and drinking? Remember to never train a rabbit if you suspect that something is wrong or if it is not acting as it usually does. Consider calling a veterinarian if your rabbit looks sick and especially if it is not eating and drinking properly.

How to teach your rabbit to jump

It's finally time for what you have all been waiting for – the guide to teach your rabbit how to jump!

Step 1: Get to know your rabbit

Before you start jumping your rabbit you need to have a good relationship to build on. Spend a lot of time with your rabbit, making sure that it is comfortable around you. The coming steps will be a lot easier if your rabbit is relaxed and used to being handled and lifted off the ground.

A good way to start if you have an untamed rabbit is to sit down with your rabbit in a pen or room and let the rabbit approach you on its own terms. Grab a book and get comfortable to give your rabbit plenty of time to figure out that you are friendly. Consider bringing some tasty treats to offer your bunny, besides carrots they often enjoy a piece of apple, salad or banana.

As your rabbit becomes calmer around you, you can practice handling it, petting it over the head, body and ears. Practice lifting your rabbit. It can take some time for rabbits to get used to being lifted off the ground as it is very unnatural for them. To make them more comfortable, make sure to always lift the rabbits with two hands, one under the chest and one supporting the back feet and body. Gently place your rabbit against your chest so that it feels secure. Make sure to never lift your rabbit by the neck or ears!

Ideally someone has been handling and petting your rabbit from when it was just a small baby, but if not, try to start as early as possible. A good relationship with your rabbit is crucial if you want to have fun together and it makes the following steps that much easier!

Step 2: Harness your rabbit

When your rabbit is happy with being handled and lifted and doesn't get startled by you walking around it, it's time to get it used to having a harness on. Make sure that the harness ties around both the neck and the chest of the rabbit. An easy way to start is to put the rabbit on your lap, make sure it is calm and relaxed, then gently but the harness on. Adjust the straps to fit your rabbit, it should be firm so that it doesn't slip but not too tight around the neck. Then let the rabbit get used to the harness on its own while running free in a pen, room or in its cage. Usually the rabbit accepts the harness very quickly, as long as it is correctly fitted and feels comfortable.

The next step is to connect the leash to the harness and take your rabbit outside of the pen. The leash should be connected to the chest strap of the harness, this way your rabbit will feel more comfortable with less pressure on its sensitive neck. To begin with, just quietly follow your rabbit where it wants to go. Try to avoid tugging on the leash, especially in the beginning. If you really need to stop your rabbit, try to do it as softly and gently as possible by carefully shortening the leash and putting your hand on your rabbit as soon as you can to take the pressure off the harness. Some rabbits can get startled and panic when they realize that the leash is holding them back, so this step requires some training and patience. Remember to stay calm at all times and try not to run or chase behind your rabbit as their flight instincts can be strong when they get scared.

When your rabbit is used to walking around outside in the harness, doesn't mind you walking quietly behind it and doesn't get scared when you shorten the leash you are ready to move along to the next step.

Step 3: Learn to steer your rabbit

This step is not necessarily the most important if you just want to get to the actual rabbit jumping part already. It can however be very helpful if you plan on jumping crooked courses or competing in the future. The point of this exercise is to teach the rabbit when we want it to move forward and when we want in to stop.

When teaching a rabbit the commando "Forward" it can be helpful to set it down close to somewhere it wants to go – maybe your rabbit loves its cage or maybe it always wants to run to the vegetable garden. Whatever it may be, try to outsmart the rabbit to help it achieve what you want. Give your rabbit some time and patience if it doesn't want to move, especially if it seems scared or unsure of what to do. Sometimes a gentle pat on the butt can help your rabbit understand. Make sure to give a lot of praise if your rabbit moves, even if it's just a few steps. Some rabbits are more laid back, with those you can try a gentle tickle under its back feet. Be careful though – some rabbits don't like that and can get startled instead.

Good jumping rabbits have learned to move forward when the handler steps close, without being nervous. Remember to never scare or run after your rabbit in order to make it move, this will just ruin the trust that you have built.

Teaching your rabbit the "Stop" command using the leash can also be very helpful. You can practice this by very gently shortening the leash until the rabbit can feel some resistance in the harness. If the rabbit stops or slows down, immediately release the tension and praise generously. If the rabbit doesn't stop, even after a few seconds, just release and try the whole procedure again. Never be harsh or jerk on the leash as handling rabbits requires patience and softness. Rabbits are small, sensitive animals and if they do something wrong it's because they do not understand yet. Taking small steps and practicing often but in short periods might feel slow, but in the end it will be a lot quicker than trying to force something upon your animal.

For someone who plans on competing in crooked courses, it's crucial to teach your rabbit how to turn using the leash. This can be quite a challenge and it's based upon that your rabbit knows the Forward and Stop command. The idea is that when you lead with the leash to the right, the rabbit should turn right and when you lead to the left, it should turn left. You can start by gently pulling on the leash when the rabbit is moving forward, the rabbit should now stop. Move closer to the rabbit, which should make it jump forward again while still keeping tension on the leash. Hopefully the rabbit will start looking for other ways to go since you will not let it go forward or let it stop. If the rabbit jumps left or right, immediately praise and release. This will most likely confuse the rabbit in the beginning, so make sure to take plenty of breaks and to practice for short periods of time.

As soon as the rabbit understands that this command means that we want it to change direction, you can make it a little bit harder by only releasing when it moves in the direction that you want. Some rabbits find it easier to understand if you also lead with the hand to the direction where you want it to turn. Remember to have patience when teaching your rabbit to turn, it is probably the most difficult part for many rabbits. When jumping straight courses it is not really necessary to teach you rabbit this command, so consider starting with straight courses and then later coming back to teaching your rabbit to turn later when you want to try your luck on crooked courses.

Step 4: Introduce your rabbit to small fences

Now that your rabbit feels comfortable and secure walking around in a harness it's time for what we have all been waiting for – jumping! If you have taken your time with the previous steps, it's usually quite simple to start jumping your rabbit.

If your rabbit is the suspicious type it can be helpful to place a fence in a room or pen and let your rabbit sniff and get accustomed to it on its own terms. At this point, you don't really have to worry too much about what your rabbit chooses to do, as long as it's not nervous around the fence that is a good place to start.

When you start training, I highly recommend starting with two small fences placed in a straight line with around two meters or seven feet in between. This way, the rabbit gets used to the idea of jumping several fences right from the start. It's a lot harder trying to teach a rabbit to jump a whole course if it is already used to stopping after that first hurdle.

Start by setting down your rabbit a few steps in front of the first fence and give it a moment to think. Let your rabbit approach the jump at its own pace, let it sniff and explore the fence if it wants to. If your rabbit pushes the pole down, just put it back up and lift your rabbit back to the starting position again.

If you have taught your rabbit the "Start" command, you can use that and hopefully your rabbit will move forward. If not, a gentle pat on the behind might help. If the rabbit turns around or runs in the wrong direction, gently lift it back in front of the fence until it understands that you want it to go forward. We want to make it as clear and simple as possible to do what we want, so try to have patience. Also make sure that the fence is very small (around 10 cm or 4 inches is enough to start with). Hopefully it will not be too long until the rabbit has made it over the first fence. If your rabbit really doesn't seem to understand you can carry it over. Now repeat the process for the second jump. If your rabbit jumps to the right or left or turns around, set it in front of the second hurdle again. If it has been a while and your rabbit doesn't move at all, a gentle pat can help. As soon as the rabbit goes forward over the jump, regardless of if it makes it over cleanly or not, praise generously and let the rabbit jump freely for a while. You can always carry the rabbit over if it doesn't seem to understand yet. Remember to praise and let the rabbit rest even if you lift it over the hurdle. That might seem a little bit strange, since we did the job for the rabbit, but you always want to make sure to praise when we get the end result that we were looking for. Usually it doesn't take too long before the bunny understands that we want it to jump over the fence itself.

Remember to always stay behind your rabbit, the goal is that the rabbit leads the way and you follow a couple of steps behind. Trying to tempt the rabbit with a treat in front of its nose might seem like a good idea at first, but if you ever want to be able to jump a course that method will not be effective. You want to be the one following your rabbit, not the other way around. When your rabbit has jumped over the pole, make sure that you always step around the fence – the rabbit should be the one jumping, not you! This also helps you avoid accidentally stepping on your rabbit in case it decides to turn around or stop after jumping.

Although it can be tempting, don't raise the difficulty level until your rabbit can jump over two low jumps without veering off to the side or stopping. As with all of the other steps, it's better to practice for short periods of time every day rather than spending hours at once. We don't want to tire or bore the rabbit, if we do it might lose interest.

Step 5: Increase the difficulty level

I know what you're feeling – you just want to start raising the fences and see how high your rabbit can jump already. I can't stress enough how important it is to have patience. If you push your rabbit too hard it will not think that it's fun and soon enough you will have a rabbit that refuses to do anything.

When your rabbit can easily jump over two small fences, my suggestion is to start adding more fences before raising the bar. Try with three, four or five low jumps. Does your rabbit still stay on track? Then you have done a very good job and the hardest parts are now behind you. If not, keep practicing the same way as before. Lift your rabbit back on the path if it runs off in the wrong direction and use your hands to help it stay on course.

When your rabbit can jump over six hurdles in a row without difficulties it is time to start raising the bar, little by little. A tip is to always keep the first and the last jump very low, because they are usually the hardest for your rabbit and it can be a good way to mark the start and the finish for both you and the rabbit. This way the rabbit knows that when it has jumped over that last small fence it will be done and get praise and leisure time. Instead, try raising the second and third jump to 20 cm or 8 inches. What happens? If your rabbit loses confidence and doesn't dare to jump, simply lower the fence again and practice some more.

When your rabbit can jump 6 fences that are 20 cm / 8 inches high and at most 30 cm / 11 inches long, you would be ready to compete in the easiest class called Mini. When you have built up to 8 fences at 30 cm / 11 inches high and up to 45 cm / 17 inches long, you can compete in Easy. In Sweden the hardest class is called Elite where the fences are 50 cm / 20 inches high and up to 80 cm / 31 inches long! Remember to leave enough room between the fences when you practice. This is even more important when you start jumping higher fences. Around 2.5-3 meters or 9 feet is what's recommended to give your rabbit a fair chance at clearing the jump.

I would recommend holding off on trying a crooked course until your rabbit feels very confident and stable when jumping straight courses. The approach will be the same when you start jumping crooked courses – start simple with only a few low jumps. Try to keep the turns fairly straight in the beginning so that the rabbit doesn't have to look too hard for the fences. Then you increase the difficulty level by adding more jumps and a few sharper turns until your rabbit feels confident at that level. Only after that would I recommend that you start raising the height of the fences. Remember to keep the first and the last hurdle very low at all times (10 cm or 4 inches is a good bench mark). When you start training with crooked fences it can be very helpful to go back to Step 3 in this guide and check out how to teach your rabbit how to turn using the leash.

There are two more disciplines that I have not gone over yet – those are high jump and long jump. I would really recommend for a beginner to skip those two to start, because the risk of your rabbit getting either hurt or uninterested is a lot higher. My personal opinion is that these disciplines are most suited for intermediate or advanced handlers who are good at training rabbits and are able to see where the limit is for every individual. I think it is very easy to accidentally push your rabbit too hard and if you do, it can be difficult to get your rabbit to enjoy jumping again. If you will want to try high jump or long jump, keep in mind that your rabbit will need to be at least one year old. This is very important to avoid any injuries due to the rabbit not being fully matured.

How to avoid common problems

Do:

- Train in short intervals and not too often
- Give a lot of praise and use positive reinforcement
- Stay calm and consistent
- Have patience!

Don't:

- Jerk the leash or handle your rabbit harshly
- Raise the fences too much too soon
- Get in front of your rabbit with your body or hands
- Have any sharp nails or edges on your fence that your rabbit can hurt itself on

My rabbit will not move

So your rabbit will not move an inch. It is simply lying flat on the ground and does not seem interested in the fence, in you or in co-operating. The first step in solving this issue is studying your rabbit – does it look stressed? Is it breathing quickly? Are the eyes wide open? When rabbits get scared, especially if they are in unfamiliar surroundings, they will tend to stay as still as possible to avoid danger. The first step in this case is to make sure that your rabbit feels comfortable. Give your rabbit time to get used to the surroundings before you start jumping. Maybe you can even move the fences to a place where you know your rabbit has been many times. Ideally you want to have something that your rabbit wants to go to on the other side of the fence – it could be the rabbits' house or a patch of grass that it likes. You want to make sure that your rabbit knows the area and knows where it can go.

Alternatively your rabbit does not seem stressed at all – it can be the complete opposite where your rabbit is totally relaxed and calm. If you have trained for a while and your rabbit suddenly stops moving, it is a sign that it is time to let your rabbit rest! Take that as a warning sign and make sure to train in shorter intervals in the future. If you ignore the early signs that your rabbit is tired you can end up with a rabbit that completely refuses to co-operate.

If your rabbit seems calm but is not tired from training, you can try gently patting it on its backside. If that doesn't work you can also try carefully tickling it under its back feet – that will usually get a lazy bunny moving forward. Make sure to praise any movement forward and give your rabbit a break when it did what you asked.

Keep in mind that rabbits are individuals and although most rabbits enjoy jumping when they have learned what you expect, some simply don't. You can never force a rabbit to jump so if you notice that your rabbit doesn't seem to like it even after having a lot of patience and taking your time with teaching your rabbit, you should not push it anymore. If you still want to start with rabbit jumping, then it might be time to get in touch with a breeder that specializes in jumping rabbits and get yourself another rabbit.

My rabbit sniffs everything

So your rabbit always seems to be totally pre-occupied with sniffing everything – the fence, the ground, you, the leash etc. This can be quite common especially with male rabbits, they want to mark their territory and put their scent on the area.

Usually you just need to have some patience in the beginning and letting your rabbit take its time to explore the area. If you have other rabbits it might be a good idea to keep them away from the training area for a while to minimize any exciting smells. Train in an area where your rabbit is used to being and consider leaving it in a pen with the fences for a while so that it is done with sniffing when you are going to train. Once the rabbits are trained they will usually understand the difference between "work" and leisure, and become less prone to sniffing then it is time to jump a course.

For some people, the easiest solution is to simply neuter their male rabbit if they do not plan on using him for breeding in the future.

My rabbit knocks down every fence

So you are training your rabbit and it seems to understand what you want it to do – jump over the fences. The only issue is that it doesn't quite make it over the jumps and keeps knocking down the poles.

An important thing to remember in this case is that you don't want to give any sort of negative reinforcement to the rabbit. Your rabbit is doing what you asked, which is jumping over the fence. Consider the reason as to why your rabbit is failing. Is the jump too high? Is your rabbit in good enough physical condition? Have you trained too much, is the rabbit tired? Maybe it is time to give your rabbit a break. If your rabbit is not tired and in good condition, the first step is to lower the fences. Try to make it easy for your rabbit to succeed and praise when it does. Make sure to allow for enough rest in between the rounds.

If you have lowered the fences to five centimeters (around two inches) and your rabbit still keeps knocking down the poles, I would suggest using solid fences for a while that cannot be knocked down. Keep in mind that this is a temporary solution and for educational purposes only. Solid fences should never be higher than 10 cm (four inches). This method is usually very effective in teaching your rabbit that the fence should not be knocked down, it's a way to break that habit. Just remember that there should still be no way that your rabbit can hurt itself on the fence, there should be no sharp edges or anything sticking out. A normal wooden plank is usually a good alternative.

When you have practiced with solid fences for a while, you can start changing out some jumps for normal poles again. Progress slowly with small fences until your rabbit can jump a course cleanly. After that you can continue practicing and start raising the bar again.

Competing

So you want to read more? Maybe you plan on competing in the future? In the coming chapter I will go in to more details of how the competitions work and what you will need to know before you sign up. This would also serve as good guidelines for anyone who wants to arrange their own competition amongst friends.

Official disciplines:

- Straight course – fences are placed out one after another in a straight line.
- Crooked course – fences are placed out one after another with turns and loops in between.
- High jump – one fence where the goal is to jump as high as possible.
- Long jump – one fence where the goal is to jump as long as possible.

Difficulty levels for straight and crooked course:

Level	Maximum height	Maximum length	Number of jumps
Mini	20 cm = 7,87 in	30 cm = 11,81 in	6
Easy	30 cm = 11,81 in	45 cm = 17,72 in	8
Medium	38 cm = 14,96 in	65 cm = 25,59 in	10
Difficult	45 cm = 17,72 in	80 cm = 31,15 in	10
Elite	50 cm = 19,96 in	80 cm = 31,15 in	12

How it works

During the competition, there is one judge that counts faults and one person who clocks the rabbit. The first and the last hurdle in the course are always very low (around 10 cm or 4 inches) and they are used for time taking. You can think of them as a start and finish line. These jumps are not included in the total number of jumps in the table above. If your rabbit knocks down these fences, it will also not count as faults as they are not officially part of the course.

As mentioned before, the goal when competing is to clear the course as fast as possible. The rabbit will receive one fault per fence he knocks down. The same happens if you lift the rabbit over a fence that is not already knocked down. For longer jumps it is also important that the rabbit jumps straight over the whole fence, if it jumps askew it will be penalized with one fault. To have a chance at placing, you want to have as few faults as possible.

Usually there are two rounds. After everyone has jumped the first round, the top half of the starting field or all the rabbits that have zero faults will go through to the final round. After the final round has been completed the two results are added together and the rabbit with the least amount of faults will be declared the winner. When two rabbits are tied with the same amount of faults, the one that jumped the course in the shortest time will win.

If you get a placing, or if you clear both rounds with zero faults, your rabbit will earn a promotion point. The promotion points are important if you want to be able to compete in the higher levels. To be allowed to start in the next level your rabbit will need three promotion points. That means that if you want to start in Medium instead of Easy, you will need to place or clear in three competitions. The same things goes when you advance from Medium to Difficult. Eventually, if you want to compete on the highest level called Elite, you will need five promotion points in Difficult.

For the classes called high jump and long jump the rules are a little bit different. To be allowed to start your rabbit will need to be at least one year old. High and long jump can be quite strenuous on the body so you want your rabbit to be fully grown and in good condition. As the name suggests, these disciplines are all about jumping as long or high as possible over one single fence. The rabbit will have three attempts at one height or length. If it jumps it cleanly, the fence will be raised until there is only one rabbit left – the winner!

There are only two classes for long jump and high jump – Not Elite and Elite. Everyone starts out in the Not Elite class by default. To advance to the Elite level you will need to get three promotion sticks. You will receive a promotion stick automatically if your rabbit clears 60 cm / 23 inches in high jump or 160 cm / 63 inches in long jump.

When you have finally qualified for the Elite level in any discipline you will compete for certificates instead of promotion sticks. If you gain three certificates in one of the disciplines, your rabbit will be named Champion. If you manage to do it in two disciplines, your rabbit will earn Great Champion. For three you will win Super Champion and the most prestigious one for all four disciplines is Grand Champion.

Rules
To compete, you need to be at least seven years old and your rabbit needs to be four months old for straight or crooked course and one

year old for high jump or long jump. All breeds and crossbreeds are allowed to compete and there is no need to bring a pedigree of any sort. Most rabbits can enjoy and do well in rabbit jumping but the most competitive rabbits are usually mid-sized lop-eared crossbreeds. They often have the agility and the temperament to be perfectly suited for this sport. Although the giant breeds are permitted to participate, they are generally not recommended because it can be quite strenuous for their big bodies to jump hurdles.

The most important thing to make sure is that your rabbit is healthy and in good condition before you sign up for a competition. Never bring an animal that has recently been sick or exposed to illness to a competition, we all want our rabbits to stay safe, right?

If you have a female rabbit, also make sure that there is no chance that she is pregnant. If your rabbit has recently had a litter, they will all need to have been weaned off before she is allowed back to compete.

Always remember that you can never force your rabbit to jump. If at any point during the competition you treat your rabbit badly, lift it in the harness, touch it with your feet, get in front of it or if your rabbit shows that it does not want to jump you will be excluded from the competition. The rabbits' safety and wellbeing always comes first! Try to keep this in mind when you are training at home as well.

World Records

The world of rabbit jumping can be surprisingly competitive and there are some pretty amazing world records to show for it. Can you imagine a rabbit jumping three meters in length? That's the length of a small boat! The world record for long jump is currently three meters / 9.84 feet. It was achieved by a Danish rabbit called Yaboo back in June 1999.

The world record for high jump is also very impressive and was set in the same month of June but 14 years later, in 2013. It is currently held by a Swedish rabbit named Snöflingans Majesty of Night "Aysel". She managed to jump a one meter / 39.37 inches fence! As comparison, a standard table is only around 75 cm or 30 inches high.

Your first competition

So you have been training your rabbit at home and it is going very well. Your rabbit understands what you want and can jump a course of eight fences at 30 cm or 12 inches. It might be time to start considering signing up for that first competition. This chapter will cover some tips for your first start.

Change it up

To give yourself the best possible chance to succeed in your first competitions, first make sure that you have practiced with your rabbit in many different environments. Everything will look new and unfamiliar to your rabbit during your first competition but you can practice beforehand by jumping in your friend's backyard or another place where your rabbit has not been before. If you always practice outside, it can be a good idea to try practicing inside. When you take your rabbit to unfamiliar surroundings, you can get an idea of how it will react during your first competition.

Try different variations for your fences, try longer jumps, jumps that have planks instead of poles and if possible also try a water-jump. You can make your own water-jump by using a wide plastic box that has low sides. Positioning the box under a small fence can make it easier for your rabbit to understand in the beginning.

If you are used to always training by yourself it can be a good idea to have some of your friends or family over to watch you. It will be good both for you and your rabbit to get used to having people and other distractions in the vicinity. Keep in mind that when you compete there will probably be an audience, someone might take photos, a dog might be barking in the background and so on.

Where to sign up

In Sweden you would first need to find your closest federation and become a member. Usually you would register your rabbit and acquire a Competition Journal. Every rabbit will have a personal Competition Journal. You bring this book when you compete and the judge will fill it with how you placed, if your rabbit won a promotion stick etc. The Competition Journal is how you keep track on your rabbits' performance.

Once you have become a member and your rabbit is registered you just need to find a suitable competition. Normally you will then sign up online and pay a small entry fee. You will not need to be a member or register your rabbit to compete in the Mini class, so that can be a good place to start if you just want to try out rabbit jumping. Otherwise you will start in the Easy class which is where you can start earning promotion points.

What to bring

Once you have signed up for your first competition it's time to plan out what you should bring. It can be good to have a checklist for your first competition so that you don't forget anything.

Here is an example:

- Your rabbit, transported in an appropriate crate.
- Harness and leash. Make sure that the leash is at least 2 meters or 6.5 feet long.
- Your rabbits' Competition Journal (unless you're competing in the Mini class).
- Water bottle for both your rabbit and yourself.
- Food for both yourself and your rabbit.
- Appropriate clothing, it doesn't have to look fancy but it has to keep you warm and comfortable!
- Something to sit on can be beneficial. Many competitions are held outside so a foldable chair is perfect.
- If possible it is very handy to bring a small pen so that your rabbit don't have to sit and wait in the small transporting

crate. Grids that are made for compost are very popular for this purpose as they do not take up much space and can be easily assembled anywhere. If you do not have that opportunity keep in mind that you are not allowed to tie your rabbit to anything if you are keeping it harnessed. You always need to hold the leash and keep an eye on the rabbit.

A day of rabbit jumping

To give an example of what a day at a rabbit jumping competition might look like I have included this chapter. Competitions are most often held outside on a large grass field. Make sure that you arrive well before the competition starts. You will normally hand in the Competition Journal and find a suitable spot to sit down with your rabbit. If you have brought a pen it can be good to set it up and let your rabbit out of the transporting crate. Getting the rabbit used to the surroundings is especially important for beginners because it will help the rabbit to be more relaxed and focused on jumping later.

Usually the easier classes will go first, so make sure that you find out when you are scheduled to start. Before your start you should allow for plenty of time to warm up your rabbit. Let it jump around in the harness and explore the surroundings a little bit. Make sure to be patient if your rabbit seems to be stressed or confused. Usually three smaller fences are set up next to the competition course, so that you can practice jumping them a few times with your rabbit before it is your turn to start. This can be very beneficial for new rabbits to help them understand that we are expecting them to jump now.

When you have warmed up you will be called to the starting line. Either hold your rabbit in your arms or hold it gently on the ground and wait for the starting signal. If you accidentally start before you have been given a signal you will be penalized with one fault.

Once you have cleared the course you will need to wait until the rest of the starting field are done. After that the rabbits with the best result will go through to the final round. After all rounds have been finished and the results have been tallied there will be an award ceremony. The top rabbits will receive a promotion stick in their Competition Journal and prizes will be handed out. Remember to pick up your rabbits' Journal after the competition is over!

Don't be discouraged if your rabbit didn't quite perform as well as it usually does at home. Your goal during the first competitions should be just to get through the course. That is an achievement in itself for a beginners. The more you practice and the more you compete, the better results you will get.

Building your own fences

Maybe you have been practicing with your rabbit for a while and the make-shift fences just are not cutting it anymore. Building your own rabbit jumping fences is both easy and fun! A few basic jumps can be good to start with, but only your imagination limits you when creating beautiful and interesting fences!

A few basic guidelines to keep in mind before you start building:

- Nothing should stick out that can harm your rabbit. It can be tempting to use a few nails to rest the pole on, but that can be potentially dangerous. Large staples are much safer and perfect for thin poles.
- The poles should be able to be knocked down from both directions. This way your rabbit will not get hurt if it suddenly turns around and jumps back over a fence.
- Wide fences make it easier for your rabbit, around 60-70 cm or 2 feet is perfect.
- Steady and stable fences will make your life easier! Make sure to make the bottom foot part wide enough. That way your fence won't fall over as soon as it gets a little bit windy.
- Make sure that the fence doesn't smell strongly from paint or solvents. If you decide to paint your fences, let them sit out in the fresh air for a good while before you start using them.
- Small plastic PVC pipes are perfect to use for poles as they are so light-weight. Round poles made out of wood are also a good alternative. If you want to change it up, you can use thin wooden planks for some fences instead of poles.

A few last words

I hope that you have found this guide helpful and informative. This is how many competitors, including myself, train their rabbits successfully. Most rabbits enjoy jumping once they understand what you want them to do. If you have gone through this step by step and your rabbit doesn't seem to enjoy jumping there is no point in forcing it. If you really want to continue within this sport, then your best bet is to seek up a breeder that specializes in jumping rabbits.

Remember that jumping high or winning prizes are ultimately not that important. The goal is to have fun with your rabbit and find something that you both enjoy doing together as a team. I hope that jumping will prove to be that activity for you. Good luck!

Photo by Emma Lundqvist

Thank you!
Thank you so much for spending your time reading my book. If you enjoyed what you read and found it helpful in any way, would you please consider leaving a review? I read and appreciate all of your feedback as it not only helps me improve, it also helps other readers to make an informed choice when considering to purchase this book.

19428418R00023

Printed in Great Britain
by Amazon